SAVARIN

POEMS BY

RICHARD WILLIAMS

Ardis / Ann Arbor

Copyright © 1977 by Ardis,
2901 Heatherway, Ann Arbor,
Michigan 48104. ISBN 0-88233-196-5.

CONTENTS

PART ONE: MONOLOGUES

    Savarin 11
    The Fable of the Airplanes 16
    The Way It Is 18
    Rita Rio 20
    Monologue of a Man of Seventy Years 22
    Émigrés 23
    Damascus 26

PART TWO: DIVERSIONS

    Night 29
    Experience 30
    Smoke 31
    Coming from a Place I Dont Understand 33
    Measuring 34
    Acts 35
    The Public Market 36
    Grey Shale 37
    The Future 38
    Labor Day 1972 39
    Selves at Play 40
    Nizhinsky 41
    The Revolutionary 42
    Mildred Sam and Henry— 43
    Equations 44

Childhood 45
The Palace 46

PART THREE: OCCASIONS

The Fop from Norway 49
Passages 50
Docked 52
Invalide 53
Debacles 54
Earth as a Planet Needs Tending To 55
Apples and Other Vegetables 56
Later 57
In May Is a Delight 58
Well 59
One 60
Coin 61

SAVARIN

PART ONE: MONOLOGUES

§ § § *SAVARIN*

I
Take one chicken from three to five pounds,
coming home from an evening on the town,
salt it with garlic and pepper,
then melt one-half stick of butter
that signals the end of it
in a pan with one spoon of tarragon,
all that there was,
our civilization,
and three-fourths cup white wine.

Stuff the chicken with the green ends
of spring onions, pour on simmering mixture
hot in the memory
from the pan, then cook
what seethes on the brain
in a moderate oven for forty-five
passing in sequence
minutes plus ten for each pound if cold
like time on end, like scallops
and seven if at room temperature. Serve

with risotto and haricots verts
on the beach
à maître d'hôtel. White wine.

II
Marinate two veal chops, rather thick,
where is my youth,
with the juice of two lemons, garlic salt,
where did it go,
and one teaspoon of crushed thyme. While
the Lord
in the marinade, sauté one bell pepper
speaks of His passion
and one onion, diced, in one-half stick of butter
as if it were a nail just bolted
until tender. Remove the vegetables
to my neighbor's eyes
and cook the chops on top of the stove
I hate them
in the butter residue for fifteen minutes,
let them go blind
turning them once in the meantime,
those fools.

Add the vegetables along with one can of
hate, but with
tomatoes to pilaf, and serve with a rosé
piety.

III
Where are the snows of yesteryear,
in one-half stick of butter sauté three crushed*

*(garlic cloves, one tablespoon of sweet basil)

goons who have besieged me
one-half teaspoon of oregano, and one teaspoon
                                        of parsley
   with their angry looks.

After ten minutes of slow simmering, add
an eight-ounce can of minced clams;
allow this to simmer for five to ten minutes

or is He?
and serve over spinach noodles.

White wine and perhaps a salad of bell pepper
I've often wondered
and tomato; tarragon dressing.

IV
Especially coming home late when I
lather a three to four pound rump roast
with garlic salt, pepper, and marjoram,
sear it for a few minutes on top of the stove
speak of love
with high heat, being careful to brown all
sides. Surround with three sliced onions
their beautiful backs
in butter
and one-third cup of water,

then cook for twenty-five minutes per pound at 325
times I've seen Satan, too,

under a tent of aluminum, and serve hot with
devils by his side, eating
baked potatoes, sour cream, a tossed salad,
pigs-feet,
and a hearty burgundy.

V
For each one-half pound of steak, cook one-half
the pain
a bell pepper, one-half of an onion
makes for a winsome frolic through bus terminals
in two or three tablespoons of butter slowly
late at night
until tender. Slice the steak into thin strips
when only the masks are out
and marinate with enough Worcestershire
to make me quiver, and
to coat each piece evenly and sparingly
dream of them.

O Jesus!
Salt and pepper the vegetables and the steak.
I've been cold too long.
Remove vegetables from the pan and cook
past my prime
the steak in the butter for a few minutes,
I've written books on religion
then add the vegetables, stir a few minutes
to see visions
until just done, still slightly rare, and serve
topped with a quartered tomato
over rice. Red wine.

VI
For dessert spread a mixture of melted butter
over the hands
and honey over toast; serve with coffee and tea
then look at them
and light up a cigarette, or a cigar
or their host.

§ § § THE FABLE OF THE AIRPLANES

Sometimes when I look in the mirror over
                                   the breakfast table
I think I'm invisible. I think this when
I am alone and not working on my airplane models. But
I do not look in the mirror when this happens. It is
all I have and my wife would laugh at me if I told
her I thought I could disappear but couldnt afterall.

She's at the store now buying some glue for my airplanes.
I have built more than a hundred and they are all an inch
long and half an inch high. My wife is keeping
                                 them though.
I am afraid to look for them, since she told
                                 me I better not.
I asked her if she was so quiet she wanted a divorce
but she only smiled and took the airplane I
                                 had just finished
and put it with the pile.

We had a child who used to like my toy airplanes
but he was put away when he was three
and we havent seen him since. The doctor said
we will have to put him up for adoption and when
we told him we wanted him back he said no,
                                 that he had proof
of something.

My wife will be home soon and will bring the sausage and

orange juice we will have for supper. I am so hungry but
I'm not supposed to go into the kitchen
                                    until she gets back.
It is a rule. I used to feel it was a stupid rule
but one day I found out it wasnt. I went in
there and saw her come out of the mirror that
hangs over the breakfast table with one of my
airplanes crushed in her fist.

§ § § *THE WAY IT IS*

It is not human to make demands on other people.
My wife should know this but she doesnt. She comes
to me while I am sleeping with a hollowed-out television
over her head and screams "Kneel!" and makes me
bow to her life as a television personality. And on into
the night screaming "Banzai!" until I contort myself into
a small island in the Pacific on which she is marooned
and where the water is rising fast and on until
I turn myself into a dashing lieutenant in the Coast Guard
who saves her and later ravishes her on the ship,
which is my left leg.

I do not understand my wife, but she has told me
it is not my privilege to question her. She has even
said that this is her love for me, that she loves me very
much, and cries sometimes that I will leave her, even
as she is standing on my body in a pair of snow-skis
pretending I am a mountain slope, and screaming "Fore!"
I have razor rasps, but these are the things that make
our marriage work, she says.

I have seen a psychiatrist about all this but he
only stares at the wall and says, "You and your wife
are acting out, which is very good." And then he laughs
and says he will see me next week and rings a little bell
hanging from a bust of Freud's nose. But
                                          he does not know
I am playing his game all along, even as I play

this game with my wife, and one day while all four
of us are in his office, as my wife is screaming "Chink!"
and is laying railroad ties across me, and as he is dying
with excitement and is hitting his little bell with rapid
movements of his left fist, I am going to leave the office
and move to some distant place
where they will never hear from me again.

§ § § *RITA RIO*

Next to me is a radiator
fluting steam. It is my friend
and I call it Rita Rio.
I have painted her day-glo
and I have placed a black light
in my mouth so that when I talk
to her she lights all up.

It is hard to screw her though.
Sometimes she's too hot.
And sometimes she's too cold.
But mostly she's just right.
I use a wool rubber.

At night, especially at three a.m.
when the beer's all out
I put cheese and crackers
under her tits
and in the morning they are gone.
Rita has nice tits
and sometimes I eat them.
They are nice.

But most of all I like her soul.
She has mystery, a perfect woman
who always loves me.
She has her moods
but I can take them.

She is all I have
and I love her through the night.

§§§ *MONOLOGUE OF A MAN OF SEVENTY YEARS*

It is dark and there is silence.
Sometimes I play old records on the phonograph
I have borrowed from my landlady
but tonight all I can hear is my heart.

Once I could pad the silence with hope
and dreams of distant roads
but now it doesnt matter
and I love it more than the sound
of my ageing friends who click the gold
in their teeth and move in death.

I have my dinners in my room and sometimes
with the woman from Cuba who speaks
in French about her ancestors in Spain.
But mostly I dont. I like to watch the ice cubes
melt in my glass, and then I know it's time.

Once I had a wife but somebody told me she was dead.
But there is a lot I dont believe. She left me in a storm
and didnt come back. I have waited
and now I speak in tongues when I dream.

§§§ *ÉMIGRÉS*

'Allow me to introduce myself,
I amp Rugert Diptsch, third
Pid of Bosnia. I write
national beast epic of my
country wiss pig and horse,
which, unfortunately, charac-
terizes history of my country.
I weel now recite two lines
of my beloved beast epic and
zen translate into your unfor-
tunate languich: "Perinski
vooie chepatski eet, berunski
ipt katorski peet!" wheech, you
see rhymes; and now for a trans-
lation to your malignid English:
"Goose went down to county fair,
to see what paté fois was."

It was 1932, I remember, when
my fater was kink of country and
decided it was depression so he
got country to build torist hostels
for de people cump to, and got
all dees magazines to it advertize;
of specialty was de national food
of my beloved country, pinsk, which
is combination of sour creemp, vodka,
and coffee grounts. It was success

until six American torists drop dead
in six weeks of bad stomachs so papa
close down hostels and turn dem into
hompes for national and beloved beast
my country, pik.

When zee communists invade my country
1926 wiss agit-prop, all dee peasants
would not do deir jops, such as retrieve
in stealth of night de soil from
neighboring Serbia, Herzegovina, and
Montenegro which had been pushed over
border wiss flood that cumps once a
year in sprink. So my fater command
de ones who would not do dis to raise
deir hants to spirit of Lenin, and
when dey did, he shouted, and militia
swept through, and cut off all deir armps.

Another time, during great sprink flood,
a ting you in your country call tornado
cump from clouts and swept over peasants
in fields as dey worked and dey all ran
to caves tinking it was de finger of God
and so my fater was loss what to do and
got the prime minister to go to Atens
to see archbishop and tell him we are in
trouble, and archbishop refuse to do any-
ting so prime minister commence to strangle
him, and archbishop say "How much? Stop
dees what you do." "Two tousand drachmas."
"I weel do eet, but leaf your fingers away."

But archbishop was angry and had plan untold to prime minister, and when he got to loud speaker microphone dat was wired to all de caves, he said "People, in de name of Got! Cump out de cafes, dot was not de finger of Got pointing to your dampnation. Dot was the PENIS of Got looking for a new VIRGIN! Ha! Ha!" and so he ran to plane which was nearby in a field of lambps and spet back to Atens while my fater was pullink his hair and screamink and do you know to dis day, dere are old maids liffing in dose caves, praying, I am sure, every night for dat to happen. But as my fater, who is now dead, would be to say when de electric light flicker, "fantsi fooie flit," which means "look out, dat bird is flying wiss no winks!" '

§ § § *DAMASCUS*

    Where was I there in forty-five when I was in novelties from Damascus where are you in this world the kef is in the pipe but as I was saying the folies were in Cairo when the war began from Beirut I remember Hasib who handled all situations yes thank you this is very good it reminds me of her lips then Hasib brought in and in the currency were novelties from Sudan the black market in those days a term of blood and then "my brother" he said "I have a delight for your eyes" I looked at him and smiled "This comes my brother from a dissolved harem the absolute of indifference an apricot tree you my friend" and I said no I do not want I and a movement of scarves was carried in on the evening the scent of palms was a backdrop for expectations and then they opened the scarves an arm the most sensuous I had ever seen the rival a sneak from behind a curtain a dagger at nightfall dripping surprise and then a legend my passions grew and the quench was more she danced each clasp was more the castinets her fingers a beauty the sun's color and then she brushed my body a scarf fell a rose so delicately placed I was in I thought hashishin so placed I could not reach my flesh the gyre about the rose I could not reach that rose contained eternal soul I reached at night that amazing night the ruby of all desire

PART TWO: DIVERSIONS

§ § § *NIGHT*

Tonight it was warm October,
the type of tray that
Indian summer has
when it brings in longing
like the head of John.

§§§ *EXPERIENCE*

Take it from me,
an idiot might be kind
but man if you go off
on one of those tangents
that idiot is going to make
up reasons not to see you again.

§ § § SMOKE

I saw her in a bar.
"Ball and Chain" was playing
in the background.
Her hair, the look of cotton
in a nest of robins,
dropped about her eyes.

"What do you do for a living?" I asked,
setting my drink next to her finger.
"I live," she said. The music stopped,
a man next to her called for a beer,
and she looked up and blew smoke
to the ceiling. "What do you do?"

"Nothing. Why dont we get out of here,"
I said and lit her next cigarette.
"I know what you mean," she said,
"there is something about this place
  I dont like."
The man next to her drank up
his beer.

"Then let's go," I said. "No, you see,"
and then she stopped to look distant again,
"you see this man next to me is my brother
  and excuse me if I'm blunt but we're
  Siamese twins." "Oh, I didnt know," I said.
"Yes," she said, and shook her hair,

"it's something I have to—how shall I say?—
live with." She pulled up her dress
and showed one leg. The other
was in her brother's pants.

"I have to go," I said.
"Sure."

§§§ COMING FROM A PLACE
I DONT UNDERSTAND

Crickets fly
into their bodies
the music is spent
night hangs over me
like sodden bread

the room is full of rain
sinking
like sand
into a grave

slow
waves of night

a current of wet leaves
runs through my body

§ § § *MEASURING*

The city has hoarded wolves
is tense by day

I want to say I am
contempt
in the face of ice
silence
in the teeth of darkness

No matter where I step
I trip into night

the memory of a dream
the shallow red
of a moon surrendering
my body

to a vanished summer

§§§ *ACTS*

Bleak night and tomorrow no end.
What ties can be cut, what memories
tugged into yesterday and left
like smoke in absent rooms. No-one.

(If the answer were a god,
would you stare into his fist;
such mystery in a smile,
such movement into grace.)

No-one. How odd that sounds.
Half-smile. Half-lilt.

§§§ *THE PUBLIC MARKET*

You must help me, god,
or else you're just a bone
tacked to the sky with nails.

What have I prayed to for so long,
if not for where
the promise ends:
the bend of a past, the crunch
of a future, the sun that will
tickle my tongue:

I am the public, their market
of belief, some excuse to live,
some excuse to engender. I am
their eyes, their excuse to kill.

Lying here without love or words
or the warmth of the sun,
I cannot face the means
to start, some slag of flesh,
some forgetfulness.

§ § § *GREY SHALE*

That summer you left
I stared at the walls,
blue stucco stained with smoke.

I thought of you:
a gathering cloud, grey shale,
fathomless blue,
afternoon
to pummel the evening heat.

Crickets rose
on the still wind,
their echoes of lightning
in distant clouds.

§§§ *THE FUTURE*

I am standing in front of my window
with the shade drawn

The future is on the other side
but I have a fear of seeing
just what it is

An occasional light flickers
through the brown paper

I dont want to see it

§ § § *LABOR DAY 1972*

Across the street from my new apartment America has lavished my eyes with the products of democracy: a police car, white, with blue lights, a car-port, several small businesses several decades old, and a number of beautifully green, beautifully early September bushes, some trees.

I would like to meet you, I would like to talk to you, tell you things your presence would make me make up, smiling all along. You look so bright, so energetic, so wistful with imagination, it would be wondrous to kiss you.

From my bathroom window with its windows that are European, I can see an old church and the North. Sometimes when I look out the window I imagine a storm approaching from the North, and the low-hanging cold falling in on swift winds behind it.

§§§ *SELVES AT PLAY*

Why commit yourself to a self; it is much better on winter afternoons not to be a stone; but to be a word spreading the imagination through other selves, who love and will look into your eyes alluringly, as if they have the secret.

I have watched her caress the corridors where we work with her costumes from the thirties; she has blond hair and plays the starlet superbly; when I see her I smile and her face goes into the snout of a ruffled cat; and she, I know, imagines then I am Adolph Menjou in spats and cane, come to offer her a contract in film, or a love entire.

§ § § *NIZHINSKY*

What did I do to turn you so against me?; they tell me your paranoiac conclusions have reached new limits: yesterday you ran up to G. in the Library with a copy of Nizhinsky's diaries, shouting "He's derivative! He's derivative! Everything he's written derives from these!"

So what.

§§§ *THE REVOLUTIONARY*

More than anything I was confused.
You choked, said you were going underground.
Your shoulders were hunched; your finger
pointed nowhere. You never wanted
to see me again.

I smiled: those times I'd come to your door
score-eyed with paranoia you'd say
there were ways to defeat the order:
die with it; be reborn to a new consciousness;
and you'd stare at the door that led to your study,
private where you kept your papers and your axe.

I'm cutting ties with everybody, you said.
Dont ask why. I never did, figured it was you,
just you, and the state of some secret world
deep in the hole of Missouri
where the new order lay low to flood Saint Louis.

§§§ *MILDRED SAM AND HENRY—*

Take it from me Mildred—
that despair you describe so fondly
just might be a claw
moving up over the sofa back.

Take it from me Sam—
those nights of Angst
just might be hammers.

Take it from me Henry—
that horror
between your eyes
just might be a clubfoot.

And take it all together Mildred
Sam and Henry, take it all together
and form a commune:
Mildred you could let
Sam beat off the claw
while Henry you could stomp it out.

§§§ *EQUATIONS*

Imagine the room whose windows overlook the sea.
Around the room is latticework.
In front of one window a man
is puffing a cigar.

Beside him is a woman on a bed.
She has a wet cloth over her eyes.
"Nada es nada," he is saying.
"Nothing is nothing."
"Todo es todo," she is saying.
"Everything is everything."

Now follow the arch of her arm
as it droops to the floor.
A rat is nibbling her thumb.

§ § § *CHILDHOOD*

Seven is in limbo after six.
Seven ways, seven lies.
The seven sixes of a game.

At six the dinner plates are laid,
the seven friends who come to eat,
the seven spoons, the seven soups,
the seven sixes that sound the rack.

A child of seven, a brother six,
the alley and the passageway.
The books are left, the twilight sinks.

§ § § *THE PALACE*

I
As we ascended the stair to where the nightingale sang,
a long rip went up her stocking.

"It doesnt make any difference," she said.
"There is no god to seal it up."

She left it for the seamstress.

II
Two clouds lay down on a plain of cups.
Through them an occasional mountain peaked.

"Those are the peaks of your childhood," she said.
"Leave them."

III
The wisdom that all things
imper*fect*.
Nightingales do not sing; they sit.

PART THREE: OCCASIONS

§§§ *THE FOP FROM NORWAY*

In his forties,
or in his teens,
depending on how he felt,
he pranced like a gazelle,
an English teacher from Norway,
aboard the lurching ship
on its way to America.

"Oh God," people would say
when they saw him coming,
"here it comes." But he didnt care,
pretending he couldnt speak the language
and saying "The weather it were good, no"
ingenuously
and bowing slightly with a grin.
The ship was his, he thought,
and he was on his way
to a rakish USA.
And if a scarf fell, he'd pick an attitude
between Garbo and Harry Truman,
saying "Allow me, god damn."
Nobody knew who he was.

§ § § *PASSAGES*

I
Past houses
each with a ghost,
we wondered where we'd be
when the sea-wall broke.

II
Silk evergreens,
a fresh wind that blew
in a bondless sky,
the flavor of love
and stew on the stove,
people storing potatoes
and being kind.

III
The girl just five,
the boy just six
who believed in life
after death because
a crushed ant smelled—

just us
in that damp house
in the country

where the late cold slipped in
from the sky.

§ § § DOCKED

Let me hear Le Havre in your voice,
the sigh of contentment at knowing it all
beneath the pitta pat of slow Gulf rain,
the swoon of brevity in which is wit.

I want to feel the madam's satin curve,
the huskiness of her direction, moonlight
and a wave of smoked air over her bodice,
laughter as it swivels in the yellow light.

O life, gambling on a break that never comes!
Where is the train that crossed La Manche
at dusk? In the rouge high as the waves licked
the image of chicoried coffee and croissants...

§ § § *INVALIDE*

Friends fall apart and go away.
But why hold on. The rose twig
relies on its thorn.

Down below an occasional whistle
falls into the wet air:
in the imagination love is more
than the beloved, jewelled orbs

surrounded by light, blue on blue,
beauty so quick the sky tips.
But the grey whistle and the call
of the sparrow: across the way

is an ancient church by which little
cherubs go home from school. Today
I'm waiting on a friend, her closeness
by my bed, and the sky will break.

§ § § *DEBACLES*

A specialist in the lore of the Soviet
and in the cookery of New Orleans, his
father a cotton merchant, his mother a
silent matriarch from whom he rebelled
when he went off to school to study
debacles, a fascination that combined
with his brusqueness gave an intensity
that allowed no flaw, and he knew women
of such beauty it was a wonder he was alone,
but he was, and it was rumored his dream
of intelligence had driven him to a city
filled with music on mild breezy days,
which along with secrets is inhabited by clouds.

§ § § *EARTH AS A PLANET NEEDS TENDING TO*

One cant love without fear of exposing
tender parts to pain, nor can one leave
love to feeling incomplete, to make sense
from pain, never-ending, like glare.

As cities drain themselves of love, love
lives on in suburbs where wry
decanters dream of haunts, grow up tough
and unaware in a field of aging brick.

Now when Earth as a planet needs tending to,
the bushels of waifs need love, and in the
forests where man has placed his soul,
 brooks murmur in the leaves, apples bud in droves.

§§§ APPLES AND OTHER VEGETABLES

Apples have beautiful lives.
They grow politely on trees
like quiet urchins, knowing
all along they will be plucked.

Apples, like all vegetables,
smile when they are eaten,
knowing their Divine Spirit, the Deva,
will pass itself on to other trees.

And the process goes on eternally,
as if some patron of the arts
with mountains of money is in charge,
so the lowly apple seethes with

the energy of the cosmos, is eaten,
and then moves on, delighted to be,
to have been, a morsel for delight.

§§§ *LATER*

There's a lot more to circumstance
than meets the eye. What did you
say? Celeste Holme just walked in.
There's LeConte de Lisle.

Paris in 1952 must have been a mark
up from an earlier period, say
1327. I am fond of trying.
Is there no success?

These are basic hors d'oeuvres.
These are squid soaked in pickle weed.
How can I be certain I have the right one.
There are so many to choose from.

Last night the stars were loose:
the captain shouted to the ugly.
I was amused by the trellis
near the moon.

A flow has started,
and from the west
great clouds loop
to form the moon.

What is formed, is formed,
and the way I look at it,
this isnt malaise;
this is regret.

Ask me again tomorrow.

§ § § *IN MAY IS A DELIGHT*

I have just finished doing fifty push-ups.
My abdomen is decreasing.
Last night I drank one beer
and two bottles of wine and pretended
I was from Bosnia, reaching
into an unconscious trough where
pigs feed on lilies.

I feel so fresh. Shortly I will take
a bath, the best of my life recorded.

§§§ *WELL*

I gave up feeling bad
this afternoon, lay on a bench
in the warm October sun,
felt the sunlight open my spirit,
become it, not attached but open,
as I was happy, thinking that you
would come along, stay a bit,
then leave me happier then to be
alone, watching others in the park.

§ § § ONE

They do that because they're bored,
you said, in reference to, and in your eyes
I saw swimming a desire to leave not so much
my presence, which was only a bit, but also
the house, the town where nothing much happens
(does it anywhere), the East, the country, and
even the planet, which you said a lot of people
are thinking is a mistake, what with the end
in view and a lot of them already having left
their bodies, the way they live.

I didnt want to say I felt brought down
by your chatter: it was Sunday morning
and the clouds made it seem infinite,
that it would end with Monday, and in a day
or two a sunrise, which is to say change.

The sunrise, knowing now as I do
that love only exists in reverie;
the imagination as all there is;
but even that I must do alone,
since to be around you I realize
the finality of your body, how it's
growing older and the only thing
that makes me love it is the sun
and projecting you into it, and loving that.

§ § § *COIN*

I

In 1900 they came like trodden fools
from the land of harlequins to amber
America, Vinland of contrasts, Mo-
hawk arrow, beaver, and bear. But
they didnt know what ambiguities
going back millenia would turn into:
wasted minstrels and lolling damsels
who with uncertain love would sit by
riverbanks in summer to dote on flowers
and the dappled birds as a cool breeze
blew in from the north on open mouths
and picnic eyes to a meat, cheese, bread
and a bit of butter on dainty knives
cut in Pittsburgh from ore driven down
ice-blue lakes full of trout and bream.

II
In the twenties they went back
to Paris to drink and sit by women
of illusion and charm, to an art as
genuine as the mocassin, as the great
iron beams that spanned rivers; they
wandered west, hoping to meet in
Eurasia and claim it as one, Aswan,
the push of doers, the might of millions
teeming in so many contrasts: from

weeping pushcarts full of onions
to the Calvinist banks and Iowa loam,
Nebraska beauties, and Texas brick,
they wept to go back but couldnt,
so held tight their secret, shook
hands, and wrote lies so real and so
full of American Good Middle that art
came to them anon and nimble.

III
But sometime it had to break, all
the denial, all the restraint leaning
over a straight-back chair to gossip
with tea and in the night tell whispers
of evil and something, some *thing* they
could not name: a purpose maybe, but
not yet, it was after the great war
of Attrition, and the boys came marching
home to more of the same but with bands
and banners and sweethearts and roast,
something had changed and they asked why,
a question poised and planted like steel
on virgin wood three centuries ante, what
life was, and so they took to '38 Hudsons,
decanted Buicks, some Fords with rust,
white-walled, beautifully gauche, a
bottle of Jack in a mason jar, and so
to the road for an amazingly beautiful
tour de ville.

IV

And what happened, they got laid, left
legacies and died, giving the Good Middle
the broad moon from the back of a truck,
to art, the pure, a consciousness for
what was always there, kept under wraps
for centuries while the church and magnates
bought bodies but left souls, much less
the spirit, which now after so long soared
like the eagle off cliffs to the ocean
that carried them so gently over her belly,
an ego wrapped in starch now finally
scratched, joyous, naked, celebrating
a consummate in-keeping with the stars,
a world at last, and with esprit they cast
their locks to the wind, found and took
to the press of antique rites, the way.

Richard Williams was born October 20, 1944, and attended the University of North Carolina, where he received an M.A. in Spanish Literature. His poems have appeared in *Lillabulero, The Carolina Quarterly,* and *Ironwood.*